VESPERS - A MEMOIR IN VERSE

Vespers - a memoir in verse

DAVID BELECKIS

DJ PUBLISHERS
CHICAGO, ILLINOIS

To Devin and Jonah, as you create your beautiful lives.

The word "vespers" comes from the Latin word for "evening."
It's a form of prayer that gives thanks for the day.

CONTENTS

Childhood

MEMORY

From the box in the attic
generations of photos—I find
a framed baby boy sitting up, diapered,
captured in a laugh like Buddha,
and in his hands—
his first toy, first friend—
my brown rubber rabbit.

I'm old now; proud I've not lost my hair.
I recall the rubbery feel,
the chocolate color, of this first companion
apart from mother,
all mine—here
returned by a memory happiest with what
always stays the same: the yearning
to possess, to love, to belong.

THE FRONT

I stand alone and alive
over death and its silence—
yet another victory absolute
enemy soldiers motionless
not one warrior retreated
not one cries for his mother
among the cardboard remnants of their rampart
I play no bugle
the weapons of this carnage
in either hand I hold—
the red rubber-band shooting guns
Aunt Agnes and Uncle John gave me for Christmas
I utter no prayer for the slaughtered battalion
of green army men—utterly
vanquished yet again
fallen upon
this field of honor—
the living room carpet—

But today I will store them
in the attic in their box
it is time—

I must lay to rest
this boy-child game—
this spectacle—
the faded fun of it—
its warfare
accomplished

THE MAKING OF AN ENGLISH MAJOR

Sister Mary Jeanne nodded to me.
Self-possessed, I stood to read.

"David and Ann?" I read
this and other primers
over a year ago.

Page five. I glanced at Ann,
pictured very upset
pointing, imploring David to chase
Spot, running loose.

I looked MJ in the eye. I let the book
Slump to my side...I recited
"Go David, go go," with
undisguised disinterest.

Eyes, black and veiled, probed me.

"Oh, so is this how one reads a book?"
Sister then tramped back and forth,
looking wildly around the ceiling,

squawking "GO DAVID GO GO!"

Those scourges of shrieking laughs
halted time where I stood—
my wry smile
planted like
a shredded flag.

MINDFULNESS EXERCISE

I say: Everybody place your raisin in your mouth; we
are going to spend twelve minutes, in silence, eating it.

Mine chafes like
a speck in an oyster, as
a Sunday dinner, thirty years before,
comes to mind...

I watch my father, home from the last
Mass at noon,
precisely place a proper bite
of roast beef upon his tongue—
he holds it there, adds a forkful of corn...
then mashed potatoes...lays
his knife and fork beside his plate
and commences slow chewing—
swallows, sips, with satisfaction, his Lipton tea...
he does it again...
and again...

across the table
the lost child
eats fast-tastes only scorn.

Family

AT ST. CASIMIR'S CEMETERY

Oak Lawn, Illinois

Thirty years since we were here,
my father finding you in this soil
far from our family plot. *This
is the grave of my <u>real</u> father.*

I return, now, another
cousin, Margaret, found naked and
dead, alone in a clutter
of pill bottles and vodka. Her
ashes were strewn...somewhere.

Joazapas, unavowed grandfather,
you froze one December night
after grandma bolted the door—your final
rampage ebbing through icing veins.

When she and your children lowered you,
the dirt received the secret
so late for those of us whose being
lies with you, our shrouded lot.

<u>Children</u>
You left a wife and three kids
in half-life, half death.
With a foot in each, they stepped into the world.
My father quit school,
started the morning fires that winter—
an engine of duty and toil. With his mother,
he raised sister and brother.
The family prevailed over want, over need;
siphoning from necessity
work, thrift, smarts. The four grappled
the depression, reached for love,
rose to their given end—
the first taste of drink.

Father of my father, your genes murder.
Your son only mentioned you once, on vacation
on a Wisconsin lake.
His sister broke the taboo—
got sloppy drunk at dinner-table...
so Dad took me out
on the pier to break
the silence at last: *My sister is an alcoholic—*
so was my father—there was violence.
He couldn't know I had just finished my first rehab.

<u>Grandchildren</u>
One by one, they racked up secrets,
kept scores, stopped talking—
my cousins—fed by grandfather's
shotglass courage, doused fear
in a lifelong masquerade of charm,
in the right schools, good jobs, church-fed hope.

With the thwarted vigor of parental teeth
sunk in their success...one by one,
they turned into what they saw—
every bar an altar.

I was stopped by cousin Jerry downtown, Chicago,
one sultry day. His wool suit
dated, unpressed,
a noose of a tie around a grey neck,
briefcase and brogues scuffed down
to the same brown.
He said he's coming from Kent's Law library,
writing a brief.
Five million dollar lawsuit, looks good for us.
I knew he'd been disbarred for years...
then he asked for five bucks.

The last we heard from him:
his mother died—he phoned—
I'm afraid
I'm not presentable these days—
I won't be attending the funeral.

Grandfather, I found your row of stones—
all deaths of 1926—one of them
remembered today
with roses, fresh and red.

I am forty years sober.
I alone claim the bloodline.

I kneel. I clear
the grass overgrowing the sunken

flat stone. I scour the name—
and the half-life you,
to this day, bequeath.

Tevas—Amzina Atilsi—
Father—Eternal Rest.

Is that a wish, a prayer, or a jeer?
Is it me you lie in wait for all these years?

FAMILY PLOT

(my brother's divorce, 1986; my sister's divorce, 1991;
my divorce, imminent)

Mom and Dad, I am here,
standing in the narrow stretch
of grass you timelessly share, recumbent
as two flat stones beneath which you lie.
Today I clear dead leaves and read on Adele's
"In life and in death," and on Bruno's
"We belong to the Lord."
Indeed.

I recall one February blizzard I kicked
and kicked away at the snow until
I found your names
and, bitten in the wind,
That day I read to you my letter of amends,
cold and sad as mystery
you left behind.

A statue of the virgin,
her hands folded in prayer,
watches over your sleep of death

in the four family plots;
as of today, no place for me,
the unplanned baby by seven years.

I pray the prayers you taught me,
blessed to be raised by two lovers
of family, of God, of life...
but not of each other.

A perished love lies
in the earth between you
a distance dark and cold.
We never saw you
touch, laugh, share a bed...
and the sin of separating—
was never thought of.

Then, afflicted by your absence of love—
Your three children grew
to attract what they saw—
then each put asunder
their chosen spouse—

And still, under the sadness of failed union,
you transfigured for us all
with an ardor of joy and duty,
the occupation of saints—
your lifetime's death in love.

Today I say:
Keep your graves—
And one day,
throw my ashes

into the Chama River
and towards an ocean
I will escape
the rotting into bone.

LILAC

First memory of the child:
standing in the gangway filling the can
with water for the garden

First dream of the child:
my mother, across a room, struck blind
"I can't see...David, I can't see"

First death for the boy:
she picked lilacs from the garden
that afternoon in May, arranged
them in a vase, placed
the vase in the parlor,
lay down
on her bed
for a nap...
and the last
few beats
of a heart
of love

that evening,
we gathered around her lilacs.

"she was a saint," my brother said.
"we have no control," my father said,
as they carried my mother
through the door
and took her away
in a long black car—
I tried to follow—

It was all
a lilac's bloom:
fragrant as no other,
tiny petals in clusters
purple and ripe and brief
as a promise of summer

every May, I run by
trees of lilac in the park
stop and breathe in the scent,
the scent of memory's
cluster, and glimpse again—

it was then—
it was always then—

and I just ran
through the fear,
the prayer, the shape
of another
vanished year.

MY FATHER SLEEPS

This morning, dawn swept the stars
away, one by one, over Lake Elizabeth.

To be a fisherman, one must fish all day long—
a law of the lake—I was told.

Like a sleeping giant in a story-book,
my father lies athwart our wooden rowboat.

Soon, the noon sun pours July
upon my dad, me, the fish, and the languor of us all.

THOSE SUMMERS IN WISCONSIN

I remember
the sunrise walk down to the boat
hauling all the gear
still tasting wake-up coffee
the first sight of dawning orange
rippling over the laketop
right towards us as we heard
the first sounds of the morning:
soft lapping all along the shore
creaks of wooden sagging pier—
the bobbing of a timeworn rowboat
then dad jumped in—
big as the boat was long—
barefoot and balanced
in his baggy pants rolled up
to his knees as he received the
provisions I handed him
without words—oars,
red gasoline can, tackle box, lunch box,
cushions, life jackets, an empty coffee can...
minnows, worms, poles...
(rod and reel for me, ageless bamboos for him)—
then the potent smell of gas poured into

a six-horsepower Elgin motor, lakewater green,
two or three pull-starts
and a low putter steered us off
to our spots on Lake Mary...
we anchored, two as one,
into a morning that would
provide bluegills, bass, the family
dinner that night

        while still a youth,
        the time of fishing was done—
        other pastimes came to light
        other prizes were won

for many years, until I reached
about his age,
often I dreamt of the catching of fish;
up in the rafters of my garage
his bamboo poles await

UNCLE JOE: BEFORE AND AFTER

What—a banjo?
said my cousin, going through
her father's stuff in the attic.
—then, a box
of old photos—
and there he was,
youthful, comely
preserved in sepia,
uncle Joe—
banjo in his lap.

Sitting by
a ragged house
wood pickets
a crooked downspout into
thick weedy patch from which
two white shoes float up into
white socks, high cuffs bottom
an all-white suit adorning
a nubile form
lapels wide as wings
a stiff collar, a neck tied
by bold stripes

his standard

so handsome a face,
hair slick and dark
as beauty itself
his averted eyes and slight
smile might say
I'm gonna play you

A sun, fierce from one o'clock
throws shadows—his head
on his shoulder
an arm stretched
on the fence

Joe's banjo
a little sun itself—
his fingers fret a chord;
his pick, poised,
on his cusp
to rise

****

He's suited in dark now—
charcoal, grey, a silk tie
lips and eyes sealed
laid out—
his fingers intertwine
now with a rosary across his chest
his little Jesus won't walk out

in this room
in his box
tonight

his wake:
whisperings—
from lives he tore through
he's in a better place—
drink made him mean—
snickers
embalmed as usual—

the only sadness comes
from his shady clients

his five daughters
estranged

Joe's last play:
he left all his money
to the Jesuits—
to his family
a banjo

THE YEAR HE DIED

In the dream my father
appears younger—about my age; yet
he's in his wheelchair.
I push him northward up through
the Michigan Avenue crowd
over the Chicago River Bridge—
across the street
a spire, made of ice, towers
above the buildings...

Suddenly,
we are atop it—

Teetering on its slick summit—
our peril exhales into
the dark ether immersed
with numberless stars
toward the shoreline
of the Milky Way...

In a blink
we are back on the street

a son pushing father past
the water tower,
beyond ever-
encircling throngs.

GENERATION

One afternoon, I'm one of two bored teenagers drinking cokes at the kitchen table.

When Anna, my very old, very confused grandma, was wandering from room to room, shuffles up to my friend Brian, and, in a whim of dementia, having never spoken more than a sentence to him, ignores me and pours upon him, in a long rambling dramatic monologue, all the details of the story of her journey, circa 1908, from the old country to America, crossing the Atlantic, by herself, packed with immigrants in steerage, because, being the oldest of seven siblings, her poor-farm family had saved up to purchase the one single ticket to the New Land of opportunity they could afford.

She presented this epical life-story nonstop, with passion, and in Lithuanian...but interspersed enough random bits in English so we got the drift, so to speak.

About halfway across the ocean, Brian could no longer politely listen; he got the giggles...then I got the giggles...and poor Grandma, oblivious to our reaction, rattled on...shortly our faces were contorted by painfully suppressed laughter...Grandma, in unfazed intensity, rattled on...and on. And our guilty laughter went on...and on.

Finally I stood and announced loudly that *We have to go* on some pretext, just to end the unintended pathos...

but not before I heard the one final and coherent detail I remember to this day: "we knelt and kissed the ground of our new country."

Friends

FOR BRIAN- 1949-2019

How we played!
that last-second shot
by number 22
crazy-caromed—
we won!
fist pumping I leapt on your back
and you carried me
around that court
all the cheering
rang from bungalows
on our south-side block
dead-ended at the tracks—
How could we know
that all-night booming
of boxcars coupling
was Beauty herself
calling on Mozart Street?

launched—

through cars and girls
into the unreal and the too-real
stage to stage

how we laughed
at the madness
in the rear-view mirror
the foam in the steins we lifted
at Nietzsche's grave
and what we fought to learn
semesters of Jesuits and drugs
and Lincoln Park and the day
Linda moved in next door
we scored a zillion points
those years in the paint—
all we dared
conjured our rise
rung by rung up
a ladder lowered through clouds
from heights we saw
the children wide
open underneath
grown into a world
worthy of your footprints
still carried through
time and times
until the limp...
the crutches, the chair
the bed...

the call—

to come
see you off

brotherless,
I growl I hide

all these
diamonds
mined
of memory—

footfalls

echoing.

DEATHBED

The sublime is a departure. -Rilke

There is a point of no return.
We have to get there. -you

these words
rise with incense—draw
a host of presences
to this room
I read for you, just
hours past your final breath,
The Book of the Dead
through the crest
of grief's first wave

you asked
for guidance beyond
the deathbed—
now at the passage
hearing tethers us
I pray you heed these words
with the same charge
I granted yours

this your compass:

as you leave the world
of your body—
watch it burn

you wear a shirt
stuffed with our letters
the heirs of your wisdom—
watch them burn

truth—always
your radar—
led you
through the playground
of the gods of wrath
in sutra study
you deflated dogma—
an impish smile
needling the Master

diagnosed—
you journeyed at last
to your motherland

you consoled Christina,
"fear is not present here...
but sorrow is."

your laugh, that led
us through the labyrinth,
is etched in Sanskrit

your bracelet of silver
now upon my wrist

with final breaths
the words
you tried to pen
fumbled away

in the morning through
ash and smoke
you will voyage
to your merit—

a lightwave

passing
the end
of dark.

for Frank

REGAN'S LAMP

Sifting through a box of old stuff—
my first grade class photo;
up front in suspenders, tie,
crazed smile: there he was:
Regan, my first friend.

We rarely played at his house—but there I saw
his birthplace

Greeted by a dum chirp...
a parakeet perched above
a four-inch mound of droppings.

The day Madame Pudgie arrived, with papers;
a proud Mr. Regan announced
"I'm opening a poodle salon."
Two years later, her coat
all matted grey clumps,
Madame cowers under the couch
amidst empty bottles.

Snooping through his Dad's dresser
we found a fishing lure:

a naked man in a barrel—
which as it slid up,
so did an erected dick...

...and that lamp:
early-sixties "modern" its mass of white
sleeked and curved into a contorted Z;
it loomed and clashed
over all it lit.
It inspired my very first poem...
I recall two words:
plasticized and jet-age.

His Dad hung in as a printer, his Mom a waitress
"They're always fighting," said his older sister Sue,
with a sadness louder than
the screaming from the basement—
a row over the washing machine.
She was stuck with minding Regan,
snuck greasers up to her room—
one too many—then,
in a sudden matrimony,
she took Randy...
for worse.

I liked my friend;
his need left him giving, loyal.
He charmed me out
onto his wild edge.

We stood at top of a slide
I slid, he fell.
Sue held his bleeding head

As we walked to get him stitched.
I felt sorry for him,
gave him a couple green army men—
the lame ones—a marcher and the radio guy.

We gamboled along his faultline...
shoplifting, pelting, laughing with
lots of showy contempt—
more so when my Dad told me
to find other friends.

Regan bought a Rambler:
put a chrome dagger
on its column-shift—

my crazy guru
drove that blue box
off the edge
of this world
to sail on
forever waves
of the U.S. Navy.

A Catholic Life

ASH WEDNESDAY

     I

We are fat
we are lost
even the carnival just
folded up—
left town
but left,
above our eyes,
a thumbprint.

     II

Ashes to ashes:
we are all mystics:
one in life one
in latency—
given one ordinance:
Examine.

And some are changed—
the few
change often.

An infinity of events

happen in the time
of the body: the nexus
mirrored
by the closeness
of beauty, truth, of love
attained—
and recalled—
in the one future.

III
I choose to be marked
by the remains of last year's joy.
Under my feet
the hallelujah is buried
knowing I cannot turn,
can not turn my back
to the welcome that was
the wave of palms...
seasons followed—here now
in dying winter, silence
cold, dark and long,
in meager aftermath.

Where
can I turn
in this land of ashes?
I trudge the circles, ever-widening
around the tomb
where ears can still hear—
gasping—
and wafer-thin echoes
of the lost hallelujah;
and the soul recalls

a third turning before
equinox—
where place is place
and time is time, and
knows itself
as soul.

AT THE IMMACULATE CONCEPTION CHURCH BINGO

Yes—I heard it—
B-TWELVE!
My last square
Covered the bottom line!
I guess I screamed it—

BINGO!

My prayer answered!

That awesome table of prizes—

I got to pick!

right away—
one called to me—
or should I say *chirped* to me—

a live parakeet!—

bright yellow and green
in a golden cage—

I took him home
Named him—what else?—Lucky

bought boxes of seeds
and a book on parakeet care

my mom taught him to say
"pretty pretty birdie"

Maxine, our spaniel,
watched him
with jealous eyes

he pecked and rang
his tiny mirror and bell
all day long with
so much joy!
so...
I made a big one
for myself!

so please come
to our church
Sunday at 3—
And maybe you'll win
a Lucky bird
all your own!

THE BODY OF CHRIST

I'm seven. That's the age of reason. So this year Sister Mary Jeanne taught us all about our souls and sin and Jesus, getting us ready for this day, our first communion.

I feel good. I received Jesus today.

Yesterday we started with first confession —it was scary, weird, whispering in this dark closet through a little window to a priest I could barely see; but I sinned for sure—disobeyed my parents, told three lies and used a lot of the bad words David Swanson taught me, stole some stamps from my brother's collection—and some other stuff...

I needed forgiveness. The bald Lithuanian priest asked me if I'd been a good boy...well, yeah, except for the sins I just told you about...gave me three Hail Marys and three Our Fathers for penance—that was easy—so I'm all good again. Made my soul clean and ready for Jesus.

This morning we walked up the aisle two by two—us in blue suits and girls in white dresses and veils, all dressed up for Jesus. Everybody had a new missal and rosary. Everybody got a host...Jesus is in every host...in my mouth it felt way bigger than it looks—no taste but crispy. Danny Maida's got stuck in his throat and I laughed at him trying to swallow it. So Mom and Dad gave me a big party to-day... Aunts, uncles, cousins...a bunch of cards all with money—65 dollars total—the most money I've ever had!—that's a new mitt and a Good Humor every day this summer! Now it's getting dark—time to ditch the suit and tie, grab my bucket and flashlight; the backyard's been soaked and it's time to hunt some night-crawlers...cuz Dad's takin' me to Lake Elizabeth tomorrow. It's in Wisconsin but the tip of it is in Illinois. There is an old road under the shallow water along the borderline. I hear my party still goin' on indoors—out here I'm happy, Jesus is happy—no sins on my soul and gettin' lots of worms for fishin'!

BRUNO'S ROSARY

Retrieved—
My dad's rosary—

A tiny Jesus
still dying still
stretched on wood—

INRI extolled
in a silver tongue
of flame
over sagging thorns

Mary, on the medallion,
appears in the grotto
above a kneeling girl

wooden brown beads
resemble
a clot of earth—
fallow—

fingers

count

his mantra
from a forest
full
of root

remembrance

green

as a stem.

CHANGE OF MIND

The Day I Decided to become an Asshole

Yes, I can pinpoint it.

Sixth grade. Walking home from St. Adrian school with Ken Drabicki, my altar boy partner.

Saint Adrian was a sword-carrying soldier in the most powerful army on the planet.

My school was not just Catholic—it was mega-super Catholic: daily masses every half-hour from 6 am (when all the nuns attended) to 11; Sunday every hour from 6 to noon; plus weddings, funerals, "first Fridays," nightly adoration of the blessed sacrament, exposition ritual at seven and closing ritual at nine...

All this required an army of altar boys. It was a huge commitment; each weekday duty was six masses Monday-Saturday. Satan was terrified of the place—I never once saw him there.

My Dad made me join, in fifth grade, a year early. I would never have joined on my own. He was an altar boy; my older brother avoided it; hence I was drafted. For *four years*; if sanctifying grace accumulates according to number of masses attended, I and all my friends and dogs are assured of heavenly reward.

I recall many, many dark, frigid winter mornings walking to the first service of the day on the south-side Chicago streets carrying my pressed white surplice in its plastic bag in one hand, home-work books in the other. Any Teutonic Knight of the Holy Grail had nothin' on me.

So, walking along 71st St, Ken and I saw a large, elderly man slip in the new-fallen snow, hit the sidewalk hard, his brown bag of groceries scattered, a bottle in the bag broke and it was now all a dripping mess. He was shook up, but got back on his feet ok. I felt terribly sorry for him, even commented that I hope the bottle wasn't anything valuable.

Then I turn to Ken and there he is, failing to stifle laughter by holding his nose, as if he just saw some cartoon clown's pratfall.

I felt sad, I felt bad. My sympathy was emotionally very unpleas-ant. I envied Ken's response,

laughter at this poor guy's hurting and misfortune; I felt the guy's pain; Ken was having fun.

I thought about it—maybe that's the smart reaction.

I certainly prefer fun to sad; that it might happen to be at some-one's expense was a good-versus-bad quandary beyond my sixth-grade horizon...So I decided then and there to turn my little back on a zillion and a half hours of Catholic indoctrination. After all, Jesus never laughed. He never even smiles. Check out every pic-ture of him. Why, on the other hand, does the Devil laugh so often?

Fortunately, I had TEN YEARS of future Catholic (Jesuit) education laying ahead of me to sort out these confusing moral riddles.

So, remember, reader, as you peruse this, there is nothing funny about it. If you find yourself laughing, try holding your nose.

CORE CONFESSIONAL POEM

Each age requires a new confession.
And now I must forgive Dave.

I just propped open the back door, and the debauched
partygoers of self-hate stumble out,
into the morning light.

And all that has been unwelcome as detriment, all
their residue, I'm left to clean up.

I forgive myself for not seeing straight.
For missing the mark of my twenties; so late to the dance...
while consorting with all manner of creeping things.

And forgive, family, your baby...
so special, strutting through
a life of preferred treatment, squandered advantage,
undampened discontent.

Forgive, oh forgive.
Mother, Father...
You gave me eternity;
I gave you Hallmark cards.

For the finding of first love, the losing
of first love, until dreaming at last
that she slept under a spell.

I must forgive my humours:
the bilious, the rages and recipients
of rages, loved or unloved.
For the disregard of melancholy,
the uninvited guest.
For scoring the sanguine on the street.
For the afternoon sleeps that elude
the crucial; a spirit left
hanging from a low branch.

Forgive me for fingering the scale
of unbalanced love. For the glance
in the mirror at every entrance...
for naming my charm agape.

And, oh, the indulgences!...from
the 100 or so Grateful Dead shows
to nights of French cuisine before
and after the opera—
too much required to satisfy
but still I insist: the world is my spa—
and where pleasure's for sale—I buy.

Forgive my disdain of the panhandler yesterday;
for the pittance I give back.

And, of course, the hatred, the murders
in my mind of the politically other,

the arbitrary other—my crusade to slay
the worshippers of a certainty not mine.

For the wind failing to blow where I listeth.

For resenting the Mystery;
its too slow unraveling...
how Jesus crept into my bones
while I sat with Buddha—
both holograms from a fingernail.

For the times I ignored those sent to save—

Swing low, sweet absolution...

For I have raised myself, no closer to the sun
than the thickness of a shoe—.
yet here—the angels
assume shape.

So, Mercy, fix my gaze above, I pray—
for blessed clemency I attest today:

It is all grace—
as whispered through the grate:
*For your penance, say
what's on your mind.*

FATHER MAC

He's been at St. Adrian's as long as love.
Adrian was a soldier and a martyr—
like Mac—who will die
saying Mass in those vestments.

Then there's his crucifix,
atop a mess of papers on his desk.
One day it bled for him
Nobody makes a big deal about this.

Once, after vespers, I knelt,
he touched it to my shoulders.

J*S*S

Mothers push us into a world—swaddle us,
get us to believe we just need to wait

for an angel to stir the water—
then shove further—to the hour
past purity, past ritual—to dwell in the breach
where manna is served—to dare the question:

What do you want? To be cleansed?—certainty from
a word?—life on a mat? Will you take the wage

of a day of mud and spit? Ask the throngs
as they wait on the hillside,

and see him advance on the waves.
As he steps into the boat, yet another

shore is imparted—like trust in the fall
of hoped-for rain

LOURDES

From her knees and uplifted eyes
Bernadette swooned, fell
writhing to the ground of the grotto
tremors only she and the earth bore
while the people of Lourdes looked on

On hands and knees—
arms bent as if seized—
ten nails of ten fingers
clawed at dust itself
dug down into black wet dirt
then smeared a fist of that
mud across her lips
and the crowd could watch
no more in a plummet from
belief into silence
one by one they
deserted the vanquished field

Behind them
loved ones
lifted her,
led her back

to another day

Unseen—leaving there
through
the disturbed soil—
living water
springs.

THE OLD SACRED HEART
MONASTERY GRAVEYARD

We found the garden of graves—
Rows of wooden crosses
up from fallen leaves,
backlit by a waning quarter-moon.
Name, birth and death
etched the history
of the cloistered underground.

Standing beyond, his silhouette:
the statue of a monk
said to "come alive"
if visited at night.
We stood before him
at our edge of possibility...

From thinning air
his eyes lifted
from his book,
searched over beyond us
resting on the night sky—
awake for us over the dead asleep.
He met our witness as stone

transfigured into pale glow
of supple flesh.
Mouth and eyes, seeking,
greeted us with sadness...
then playfulness...
his sight swept through us—

He smiled,
light from light,
over the dead,
the living.

ON THE RIVER:

Honeymoon

Twelve of us, a flock, worshippers, my new wife
and myself on the Chama River,
our chosen honeymoon this pilgrimage
high in the southern Rockies.
On three rafts and two canoes we have steered
into the calm beyond the last of the rapids, the end
of churning, two overturnings, that roar now
a whisper through a reign of quiet.
The river wide and slow, lake-like, reflecting blue
under the sun lifting our last day into being.
Sunday morning,
swallows swoop and dart
through cliffside lifespans
as we approach the bend around which
the monastery stands in upward reach of stone
in time to prepare the high Mass for the week.
In shared vision one by one we stand,
carried on deliberate waters,
wayfarers of hope, we face
the eastern shore; the church—
bell tower and cross itself

the goal of the beckoning
which brought us from so far to so close.
We see movement ashore—
in robes of brown a monk hastens,
enters church...pulls the rope, a conduit
from this to the other world...
once, twice, nine times
the tolls ring loud and call across
the healing waters; each peal invites,
a deeper entry—communion
into this, the great mystery
toward which we always drift—
and from this refreshment
of the one tenor
our senses transform
into ceaseless gift—
over these waters,
every thought a prayer
every prayer a vow.

RETREAT WANDERING

On the ninth day, I quit my cushion to walk,
to walk slow through each moment stretched
by heat in June of Iowa sun...

A tractor droned...a monk
bent over in labor under a field hat.
Passing the grounds out back, I saw
the acre of white crosses in rows
each name numbered by lifespan—
all face west...

My feet take me
through ripening fields of corn, of soybean—
today even blue of sky itself
hot and potent—
the breeze too weak to relieve.

I cross a railroad track
its ties like footprints
vanish into both horizons.

I find, in a covert on the left,
a barricade hidden in its overgrowth—

a road one day stopped—
then slowly earth-swallowed.

I follow black bits of asphalt
splintered by relentless foliage...
further on, faded,
a "keep off" sign—a rusted bridge,
devoured by years of thick climbing vines;
under which, clear and cool, ever-seeking,
flows the stream.

Across on the right—I'm dazed to see
another—burial ground—
these tombs crammed into
a forgotten acre bound
by a falling fence
in 1944,
its last plot filled.

I step into this space,
deserted by the living and the dead,
a stranger, accruing memory.
Stones stand
to defy the disregard of time.
No shadows cast here,
under the sun at noon.

A crow eyes me and caws alarm
and jumps to a higher branch—
leaving the air closer, and
in that moment—
the tower bells
toll—

monks called to choir—
mid-day Angelus—the fourth
of seven daily chantings of the hours—

All of this—
a celestial timepiece wound—
as the sound
of comfort
for this world
and the next,
on this day
and every day
of every year.

RELIQUARY

I advanced to the reliquary,
the faithful and the curious
swirling around me all colored
in robes, polo shirts and saris,
to rest my hand
on a small glass box
with sculpted gold, onyx columns,
and a gothic roof pointing
skyward, and the remains
of Therese inside...

Then a woman's hand settled
lightly near mine
on the glass—
and touched
with grace
my eyes—

Each nail painted
in undulating lines
of copper, bronze, Carmelite brown;
three rings, fine as foil
glowed on three fingers...

her bracelets—loops of gold
over an ivory sleeve of silk—

Gripped there
my gaze ceased
its pilgrimage—

for that vision
I came—
no need to ask
for more.

SAUL

A Hologram—
Saul—means "asked for"
one bitter but borrowed herb—
at the first crossing...
both eyes dyed white—
his tent, his road,
seized—
and then zeal, zeal for law,
arrested—
horizons, past and future
sponged away—
all but a shard
withdrawn

SOUL

There's so much
we must be
witness to:

the soul—
struck
from flint
a point
red
and sent—

a particle—
coheres—
the God
we must
befriend

THIS IS PRAYING TO MARY

All of us are here in the dark—Dad too
He's never here at night—
He's "laid off"...lots of worried whispers with mom.
He sleeps by himself in a scary bedroom in the basement.
He's always working, but he took
me fishing some Sundays. And to movies.
He's at his chair, not sitting—kneeling.
His big fingers pick black beads,
with a little silver Jesus.
A rosary.
Hail, Mary, full of grace,
Mary is the mother of Jesus.
Everybody's got a rosary.
Bob has a red one. Bob's old, in 6th grade. He's down from
his attic bedroom; he used to play with me
now he's up there reading books all the time—thick books.
Marilyn, she's old too, she stares mean stares
at me; she calls herself "pretty Marilyn."
Just wait 'til I'm smarter than her.
Her rosary is glassy purple.
I lean closer to Mom on the couch.
Mom stays home with me, being mom.
Hers is green and sparkling.

I had a blue one but she took it
after I wrapped it around my leg.
My family, just shadows in the blue streetlight.
Then Dad says some words,
then the others say more words,
the fruit of thy womb Jesus.
I know about Jesus. He's hanging above the sofa
I see his picture all golden through the dark—
I watch Bob and Marilyn, they've done this a lot,
I hear them praying, praying to Mary.
I know the words. I could pray, but I won't.
Instead, I watch the squares of light from passing cars
slide around the room, this way, or that way,
guessing which way the next will be.
Mary's like Mom. She won't mind
if I skip out on praying.
...is now, and ever shall be—
The rosary goes on, I keep score
6 cars from this way,
To 4 from that way.

VIGIL

Cistercian Trappists live in seclusion and silence. At 3 am they gather in church for the first chanting session of the day, vigils. Then, every two or three hours, the bells call them to lauds, matins, sext, terce, nones, vespers, and compline. In each of these seven "prayers of the hours" one of the 150 psalms is sung.

They do this every day of their lives.

From the dark
tower the bell tolls

Monks, awakened,
walk, one by one,
as through a garden

In robes of brown and white,
each to his assigned space
two rows of choirs
face each other
in prayer, in song

All is simple here
walls of stone and
roofbeams of timber
grey, brown

The aisle parts the men,
rises to the altar and
Christ on the cross

Aside it, an icon—
two touches of color
her robe of blue,
halo of gold—
specks of sky

From the silence behind the screen—
the organ pipes a massive murmur while
voices of men fill and lift
as one in plainsong chant
deep as pulse at dawn
the fifteenth psalm:

O Lord, who may abide in your tent?
Who may dwell on your holy hill?

CLOISTER

Three long hours
after midnight and three
before dawn the bell
tolls them awake
then melts into night's quiet,
the silence of a lyre's unplayed string.

One by one, monks appear
in ancient procession
slow as pain—
some wheeled,
spines bent over walkers
throbbing joints
limping, slumping,
each aching to take
his place.

Seven times every day
these monks chant
the poems of David,
the Shepherd-King,
his Temple-songs
rage and thank

lament and praise...
and for this, all this
today seven times
they will assemble
for in all this
each hears his voice
complete a chorus
forever pregnant.

Those in the cloister
still hearty with vigor, skilled,
upright with strength,
work the farm,
polish oak and elm
of their carpentered coffins—
their trade.

I count seventeen in brown
and white robes—it was
nineteen last year—
two more small white crosses
in the field out back—
all in perfect rows
eastward facing
like soldiers sacrificed.
The grass above them
grown thick with green heat
of the Iowa sun.
This is the end
of simplicity.

But not one young man,
not one, has come

to fill a seat
in the emptying rows
reaching so far back
to the hopeful
listening behind the grate.

What can ever replace
any one moment—
of this timepiece
or this cog of diamond—
measuring only
arrival?

Hacking It

ANOTHER HORSESHIT NIGHT

barely made my nut so I
can't stop I turn north
down uptown's most
serious-crazy street
every corner
the signs say
Clark
but I read
souls seared
and shredded here
never closed

dashboard clock said 3:30 a.m.
my head said Tuesday—
time don't run out—
it just runs

a block and a half
down on the right
movement
a lone figure
flags—
a lone top-light

converges—

I felt her
hard breathing
before I even stopped
two bags full
of clothes and stuff
hair distressed
she's not high but—
an escapee—

I ask—you safe?

yes...no...
I had to get out of there—
he got crazy on me
long story—

I didn't want to hear a long story
she didn't want to tell it—
so I told her mine

she could hear,
really hear—

by the time she got out
she smiled
gave me a twenty
and her twelve-step directory—
keep it, she said.

GOOD NIGHT LADIES

Two ladies too late,
overtaken
by the salvage shift
takers, users
seventh-day losers

their dime-bag breasts thrust up
feet jammed into stiletto heels
falter across the asphalt
the Uptown Motel parking lot

toward door seven
or is it seventeen?—knock—

a mist of red
backs up in
a syringe

my tip: two bucks
and a whiff
of junk-sick
perfume

LAST FLIGHT OUT

Slow night...sitting on post 2:
Morse El stop; drawing room of
The northside,
thirst of the unfree.

I'm sober six weeks two days
still bottoming—
what's not drunk away
gets conjured.

A shudder and I'm not alone...

Take me to the VA—downtown.

He fails his small-talk screening—
angry non-sequiturs,
rambling, outrages—

I speed...grip tight a wheel—

on the present stretched out
southbound down
Lake Shore Drive.

STAIRWAY

A young waif flagged me down
just after midnight, on
north Clark, artery of the offbeat.
Thin, frail, a fallen branch
from the other side of night.
speed-freak? I think.
I chat, turn to her face—
deep eyes, deep and clear— to traces of angel-fire...
she's good, and damaged, *Cancer?*

Uptown, to a street that dead-ends
tenements with broken doors, broken locks.
She pays, tries to exit...
her body won't go—
she looks,
Can you help me?—
Sure, I say; *shit,* I think.
I scan a block dense with threat; a shadow
hurries out of sight.
I park between streetlights.
Holding her up we limp a few steps.
My goal: end this fast—so I carry her.
I feel her bones, papery skin.

We glide, swift with adrenaline—
from my arms she unlocks the front door...
"Fourth floor, sorry."

We start up the stairway; peeling paint, graffiti.
Through dim yellow of bare bulbs

We trudge,
lift thigh by thigh,
hearts beating
inside the silence.

Third floor. We halt to noises above—
then: a hard voice of a man—
Carol? That you?

Put me down she whispers.

I leave her leaning against the wall.
She lifts an arm good-bye—
I'm down the stairs,
quick as a cat I slip away,
safe in cab three-sixty-two,
back to the night,
top-light lit.

RONNIE

Her whisper of a dress rides up—
a thigh slides then another across
my back seat and
I see a poem.

then into her eyes—not
hooker eyes— but free,
blue as sky-fed lake...
their centers beam black—
all of Chicago night
invited into our cab
in mind we
commingle along
an expressway pulse

There's sex in
her laugh

We confess
why we hack and whore

I'm in transition...
well, four years now

doing time—
metered

Money's great;
my kid's at Barnard...
I could kill her deadbeat father

The meter clicks I-94

Along our boundary
we ride
gathering what we gather
until a driveway winds
to a ranch house, spreading, a field
within a field

then Ronnie slips away from me
through its dark entrance,
between veiled lights
falling from curtained windows.

THE STREET IS A STRANGE
BURNT GOD

The street is lit with bonfires
of uniforms, drudgery, bosses in effigy.
By some tenement,
"Oh, gracias, gracias—thank you thank you,"
he shook my hand again
in stupefied togetherness.
My fare, my new amigo, Eduardo
stumbles out, pulls out a payday wad—
totters, grabs to steady,
drops all his bills into
the puddle he's standing in—
"Eduardo! Jesus!..."
We're so exposed—
street-demons smell the fear—
shadows stir...
I jump into the cold drizzle
run around my cab—
he sways,
muttering,
I scramble—
scan for goons—scoop his bills—
"You OK?—there's you're casa—su casa—donde el key?"

"Ah, si, llave, si"
baffled by many keys—
at length brandishing one—
"Go!—buenos noches!"
bungling away at his door—
I and the street waiting watching and waiting...
I pray—finally it unlocks and
by the light of home,
he is lifted safely in.

Out There

TRIBULATION

I made it to the bench at night—
to frigid gusts unblocked
whipping in from over Lake Michigan
stinging fingers twist off the quart—
I gulp mouthfuls of cold—
got to get it down fast and get back fast
(told her I was just going for a cigarette)
Chugging down to near-upheavings
the churning ice-laden waves thrash
the shore—sprays freeze fast.
Drunken, shivered, I'm blown back
quaking—then,
gathering, push eleventh floor,
I maintain
a correct walk into living
room's woolen heat—
so still within our walls;
lamp lit—seems clear—
Karen on couch, nodded,
book in lap, heedless—
I pulled it off again—now,
looking out over the lake,

Snug, in the orange glow
of embers
behind the grate,
I hook into the throat
of this arctic wind.

END TIME

I remember the throb of sunup—
clothes sticking to me,
a strange room, a bottle
of cognac on the floor—
cognac, for Christ's sake—
squinting at a clock.

I remember swearing at the key...
the door swings open
I thought she had left for work—
and there she is...
I'll never forget the fury of her.
and—all this is hazy—I yelled
something back with a throat dry
as sand and we fought—
like never before—our way to the kitchen.
I gulped water but she smashed
that glass against the wall...

It all went black until noon.

I woke again to that same sun.
Same clothes. I remembered more

when I saw the floor: cracked
shatterings of clear panes,
shards of florescent glass—
my suspended ceiling—
the purse over her shoulder
and her silence
as she walked out the door.

BENDER

I wake up—here again—
daylight's wave of dread:
loathings sling through
the brain—and split—
implant in hemispheres:
fear of drinking—fear of not drinking.

A rectangle of sun seeps through
the blinds and frames my hiding
under pillows and blankets.

The morning's hours
will be mine.

I listen from my burrow—
flow of faucet, clinking of toiletries...
I smell her coffee.
I wait...the door shuts: my opening...
Like a burglar I creep
To the window and peek out.
Karen, from the sidewalk,
slows, looks back as if
hearing the distance

of a familiar moan.

I down the first
of last night's leftovers—sweet,
cold as lone-shark cash.
As lights go down
in my house of mirrors...
later—tomorrow—
next week—I'll pay
all I owe.
For now,
sink to mud
at river bottom where
scavengers fatten sleepily.

Recovery

ABSOLUTE

Needing you still I come when I can this time
down to the church basement
where we share a destiny,

like the first finders of the Way
hiding beneath the Temple floor—
strange that talk so pure
only takes place candlelit.

Here in storage, a crummy room
a circle of folding chairs, Styrofoam-bad coffee
Big Books about, blue
and beat-up as their readers.

From Park Avenue to park benches,
one by one
they stumble or strut or crawl down
the stairs into
this space filled
with the sure
and the unsure.

And here <u>you</u> are—
we've been waiting for you.

Skip the twenty questions...
let's keep it simple—
one statement—true or false:

drinking turned me into an asshole

(keep in mind—you're a liar)

By the way,
I prowled
the wrong side of night
for years—
until the morning I
woke up—
in a puddle.

If you answer right, you've just
been handed the first key;
if you answer wrong,
no god will save you.

12-STEP LUNCH

I sit across the table and wonder why we're here—lunch again, like yesterday. We sober ones know each other's all, all about the honor of your marriage; my recent divorce, my chosen celibacy. Yet we talk with pleasure of a mutual passion—French films. You remove your jacket—the outermost layer of black—and your beauty comes closer. I wonder where such loveliness goes when unseen.

We nod as we discover agreements and prolong delight, sipping cokes.

You say yes to dessert—we go to an ice cream place down the block. We share a cup. Desire longs to tell you how the tangle of your brown eyes sings into my spine. I notice these things. I'm strapped to a mast above the inviting water...I see the skulls on your shoreline...

HOMECOMING

Spread my ashes in Uptown
where god is a 4 am license
where I've been strewn
in dissipation absolute
yes I bottomed out there
hacking the night shift
roamed the zoo
of the uncaged
scratching for a mirror
ugly enough
in that recurring nightmare
of Wilson Avenue—
praying for the one
shock treatment
too many but then those
barbed-wire blackouts
ensured I couldn't see
what I couldn't see until
one morning—

a whimpering

moment

cracked—

You've only got one problem, she said

and she never lied.

OUROBOROS

It was late but
I had to run
(those days I was always running
to things, from things—
early sobriety, early divorce);
so miles of night
and miles of sweat
purging...
on a loop home
I crossed a campus—
from labored breath
emerged a humble grotto

above its rise of shrubs
under a canopy of rock
Mary stood,
as always,
arms beckoning,
patient,
silver in the dark—
the glow of collected hints:
dorm windows behind,
each lit with story;

some points above
light years distant

this moment opened
with impulse: to see
the snake uncovered
under her foot...

drawn up, I reached
through the tangle of green
and there—at her feet—
a ring—
a ring of gold

I sat there
the ring nested in my hands
I remained
in tableau, late,
late as morning sleep
reclaims
a dream.

TRIBAL

All I needed to learn I learned on the playground.
In kindergarten, I wondered why nobody played with me;
so I lost myself in toys and naps.

At school recess, us outsiders
Found ourselves—in mischief—
The fun of annoying the nuns:
the kiddie rebels.

My dad, spotting my penchant,
forced me to enlist
in the prepubescent military...
the altar boys—
deployed for three years of kneeling
in a white surplice over black cassock,
praying in Latin, ringing bells.

I graduated to the wise guys in high school—
ate at our own lunch table—around us
the jocks and the student-councilors, souls
doomed to the mainstream,
and our disdain.

When in River City,
I hung with the pool sharks.

And, of course, I later found the haven
for social maladapts—
libraries—books—
my first real crush,
the one I never got over,
was James Joyce...

Peak of my matriculation:
falling in love
with my Shakespeare professor.
She was a brilliant New Yorker
without a feather of pretense.
When no hands went up in response to her questions,
I raised mine to rescue her from
from the undergrad philistines.
Susan was pregnant by a Columbia
grad which somewhat deflected
my beams of adoration.

The logic of loneliness tightened its grip
when I hung my diploma in a taxicab...
My first day, a fellow hack said,
"Every cabdriver has a problem."
I needed nights of constant movement—
if only in one direction—away from
Travis Bickel—as I smoked and drank
and steered crashward with a tribe
of barflies practicing
suicidal voodoo...

Which led me to the Mustard Seed in Chicago
and it was there my tribe of tribes found me.
I put the one-year-coin they gave me
on my keychain...
though faded now from 40-years' wear,
I never lost it—
in my pocket—
are the all keys
to all the playgrounds
I'll ever need.

Dreams

BIRD ON A HEAD

Well, well, guess what?

I woke up this morning with
a bird on my head—
my guest!
round, wild-feathered forest-brown
her feet of tiny bones grip
this headful of greying hair—
in welcome I
move slow—to not jostle her away
for she had flown
across the skies of sleep
to rendezvous in dream.
A feat
singular as a spermcell's swim
promising as a pledge to me
this new morning—and

You spoke!—

in random ellipses of a parrot—
greetings so sweet but—from where?
learned from whom?

I received these
little secrets as kisses
whose subtleties sway
in the unversed air I breathe—
I trust—for their source circles
for me the ever-widening
worlds of night

let me paint you in words
with wings spread wide
onto the ceiling of memory
for this dawning, dear one,
you outlasted
the disappearance
of dreams.

MOVEMENTS

I sleep with a storyteller
who conceives dreams
to sift the fakery of my day away—
whispers
I dare you to be happy.

Such creation
anchors my faith
more than the books, more
than cities of revelation,
more than my hand:
a full house
of queens over kings—
more than memory—the lovers,
the rings...

I face
an intimate palette
of an old master:
a landscape and a portrait
share a wall the colors
of essence framed.

I sit, first row, as
house lights dim—
Stage Right: Enter:
the Players—Act One:
A Comedy tonight—
our masks stay on
until the lights come up—
a bow and a bid,
good morrow

Now with you I hear—living strains
of strings, the choir
sings, through clusters of stars,
a movement, christened,
by lyrics of want,
from light-years—verities
conducted for you
and I, drawn
together here—

Let us dance
each other home!

ODE TO NIGHTMARE

Stop! Stop!—this
spasm of fright
Who is it? who slithered in—
claimed me in bed
bound me in this play
of too-real dread

Why such horror
summoned from
the unknown dark
ravaging holy peace
of my quiet night?

I heard in reply—
You do not know? You wonder why?
OK—don't be shy—
in the knot of your deepest fear—
it is there I lie

look at me—look deep—
you dare to
stare me down?
do so until you see

my eyes are yours—
one in sight—
this is the source
of my hideous renown

for I am fierce as your flight
abiding as denial
do you really want to know
why I drag you to trial?

So grasp your chains you won't
shake off the dread
you keep watching those movies—
zombies feeding off flesh
in the land of the dead
for this is the tangle that binds
to my synchronous web:
you bleed
you will bleed
because...you have bled

A POST-EINSTEINIAN PSALM

A man, a suitcase, a bus stop
encircled by a horizon
of crops and sky, a midwest field
cleft only by a road
that emerges from mirage, passes through, and
thins to a point beyond.
"Country highways go on forever,"
he mused as he wiped the sweat from his neck.
middle aged, fleeing his crisis;
in a wind so slight, the heat so close.
He looked down. Ants searched the ground.
"wonder what they eat in their little desert?"

a murmur from out there—it
swelled into the hum of an engine. He spoke:
"uh-oh...'crop-duster flyin' where there ain't no crops...' "
He squinted down the road at the incoming shape, reached
for his bag, beat-up and loaded for anything.

"Tramps like us, baby we were born to run."
He enjoyed his irony; it still protected him.
He closed his eyes, listened with slow exhales to the nearing

rumble of rusted muffler and then a fume
of exhaust and dust was upon him—the door opened
he stood
squinting up at a back-lit shade, heard it call:
"You on the bus or off the bus?"
He stepped up...
"Always," a man of few words.
"Where you going?"
"Further."
"Well we're headed east."
few were the riders; he settled in
a window seat out of the sun.
"Thank God the AC works."
He leaned and dozed against the glass.

Soon, soft-shaking motion bore him into himself...
Behind fluttering eyelids, beyond the prayer of sleep
past memory and fate deeper
until he stood with his first dream of his life
on a shore of black...there
an other awoke in him...another pilgrim
adept in wider orbit—imparted in him
new vision of all
his deaths all his births in endless stream
as his mind reeled through the new expanse and
no matter where he turned or where he looked he
ran again into himself—
all within the moment
of a perfect play of light...

A pitch of the bus jarred him awake...
startled, he saw the travelers...
"...a bus...I'm on it..."

He reached into his suitcase, felt for an orange.
"Still there—good."

He peeled and ate—
its juice cool upon the tongue
and so sweet.

THERE IS A ROPE

There is a rope—stretched
between the worlds through
a molten umbilical expanse.
Each night arms with warring fists
grip and pull it taut
and tight and tighter
nightlong in dual overkill—

Then from this deadlocked span
the very breath of dreams effuses:
coheres into the field where minds asleep
shelter dormant memories—
there spawning with new light
the telling dramas of the night—
the night of me—
by apportioned strife,
concealed.

Patients

FLYER

Ben's story

One night, this Jewish kid got
drunk in the wrong hood
in the wrong joint and some
Disciples dragged his ass out
back in that Chicago alley and beat
him to near-death until
a bartender came out and stood over him:
"ENOUGH!"

He saved my life, Ben said.

...but left him with a new script:
PTSD—1943

And so, hooked on trauma, he
enlisted...bent on flying;
by 1944, he flew—
over Germany...yes, <u>Germany</u>—

"Did you know, then, about the death-camps?"
Yes.

This son of Israel wrecked the wrath of Yahweh—
bombing Nazis—over,
and over.

Ben: safe on the ground;
Dresden: in hellfire.

From his bed,
He shifted his failing body from side to back;
his eyes, lit with depth, met mine, as
he answered the question I had to ask:

"How did it feel?"

...It felt <u>wonderful</u>...It was...<u>revenge</u>!

" And... after the war?"

*I took a pass on the family business, went
to medical school...*

*I spent the rest of my life
practicing my medicine...
in third world Africa.*

He smiled.

*We don't see the world as it is—
we see it as we <u>are</u>.*

KENNY

I was warned about 324: "oriented times zero: nasty-ass;
throws food...AT you."

Dementia left his fire unattended.
His eyes flit at me.
"May I come in for a few minutes?"
"—she's not allowed there—the cunt—"
he says to the opposite wall.

Kenny—a man alone—
his thoughts locked in a sea—
where stray ellipses break like bubbles and
he assaults the air when hooked
by some vexing flotsam—
through days and nights beguiled
by horizons that were his alone.

I sifted a summerful of neural misfirings,
strung hints into themes.
A portrait emerged;
a past of renown:
Professor Kenneth T Gossett
of Columbia U;

his lectures packed, books awaited,
tenured by ivy.

Then time sunk his mind
into the quicksand of that season.
Now compulsed to re-dwell there
among remains of
before and after years.

OPEN TO MEAN STREET

A walk-in: young male,
agitated, lurking.
All in dark, hoodied—
I felt his voltage.

You a therapist?

Derek, eyes that fix and dart
and fix—takes the chair
across my desk like it's his.
My queries are soft, hover just
beyond the threats on his radar.
Some words connect, but
black lightning flares
from his distance—
shards of truth, vacancies, rants
his landlord, the courts, Rita, others—
coagulate into story

the street his mother
its speed his father

...you tell me the wrong thing...I'll kill you...

he zones into communion
with some splinter of self

I hit code grey
on the phone

mercy of the night:
cops and a psych unit bed

KATIE

Katherine, 7 month-old female;
Pronounced at 0645.
         He tells me
of his grandchild—
         brief
as a birthday candle.

Mother, untried,
         suckled
her last night—

We remain in the room
   with Katie,
         her only,
   laid in white,
      pretty, slight,
her allotted heartbeats,
used.

I see her hands,
   tiny fingers...
   Who is this
   missing one?

Alone,
in a bed for the grown—
blue of her eyes
sealed
from skies.

THE STORY OF HENRY

I visited Henry,
68, oriented x3.
He lived alone.
No symptoms
Or pain—but—

A lethal aneurism;
inoperable,
in his brain.

He moves
fishlike--
buoyant through
rooms of art
and books.

No, no god,
no heaven or hell.
There is no
fear for me...
I know I have lived.

I have left
My loved ones, my paintings,
Chelsea, my cat,
And my body,
my very good friend.

He asks
Do you play chess?

I see my hand
rise and open.
I want to win.
I want to beat
this guy
on his last smoke.

With a routine ploy
I take his bishop—
he's gazing up
at a branch
of green
brushing the window.

Check, I say.

He sips tea.

33

I met a male hospital patient shot 33 times over twenty years; an ex-gang-banger who now counsels young men caught up in street violence.

33...33...as if Jesus took a bullet every birthday.
Mickey's head sits winces as he moves;
walker bedside,
head heavy on shoulders,
Buddha-belly heavy on butt,
the bed bears his brunt—
his fat and muscles pierced and pierced
with weight beyond heft; four bullets left in him
distort the gravity and space itself, in the room, warps—
revealing, as particles do fields—
him: an island; a volcano, dormant before dawn,
arteries of lava,
from smoldering center, stream downward;
mountain of liquid light: rock returning to reef
under the light of glowing topaz.
Some brown islanders each morning sweep ash,
remnants of songs in their throats.

Then I am pulled into his eyes—eyes—rarified truefired,
fire-from-fire-eyes:
his what-are-you-waiting-for eyes burn through me—
don't waste time, our time, with non-love
eyes fierce beckoning summoning to test
yes says my gaze—
—it's your decision
I'm waiting to meet you now—
now—deep calls to deep
below the plots
of buried bullets;
now come, come and see—
there is no place you cannot rise from:
west side Chicago streets,
every fear you've ever fled—
death—
now you know
your pestilence is your own:
armed,
use words if you must...
hurry.

The Arts

DAVID AND ROBERT*

...and those, who are beautiful, who can retain them?—Rilke

We sit enthralled in the rotunda where
David is pedestalled;
his white mass
lifts us into his moment:
the shepherd descries the giant of Gath across the valley
weighted with the armor
he had shunned.
Beloved, whose eyes (beautiful eyes, it is written)
burn God's world green.
Naked, in the sea of possibility
power from
a perfect body-memory
of a lion struck dead
in the hills of his flock.
He stands ready.
His large hands,
which had soothed the fits of a king,
feel the stone,
smooth as forehead
beneath a helmet's plume.

Robert;
a self-portrait:
all black-leather,
a rear-view against sterile white—
standing spread-legged wearing
only hip-boots—
grips a bull-whip shoved
up his rectum
falls to the floor
snakes off the frame at you,
at your feet.
Light sears down
like a neutered sun,
stains one side with a shadow
of slain silhouette.
He twists to face you—
brightened curls
fall over the eyes,
placid eyes
watching you
see what love does—
its act, its work.

*In 2009 the Accamedia Museum in Florence presented its first modern art exhibit ever, a Robert Mapplethorpe retrospective. Its placement adjacent to Michaelangelo's *David* provide a startling and delightful experience of juxtaposed artistic visions across centuries and cultures.

A DREAM

matchless, this visit
from Starry Night
two dimensional,
soundless,
I face a wall
a painting hangs

a landscape—of lovely
Provence summertime
rendered as dissolving and
arising from formative
waves of a sea of possibility
into a prism of new
lavender greens and swirls
of sky in many blues. Over
and into all of this the sun
in yellow sway
impresses upon me
the moment and work behind
the curtain of creation
eyed with lucidity
of the master.

an homunculus appears;
all in white, ghostlike
he floats up near
the center of the scene
and hovers there in
a space he knows to be a portal
and in a slow dissolve
he inserts himself
into lifegiving splendor
into the colors
he had brushed
long ago.

MOVIEGOER II

I had trudged through the "real world" into a seeming adulthood. Then, in just two hell-years, my dad died, my wife left me (and took the garden and the dog with her), got fired for the first time (from the best job ever), tried teaching high school girls, (the worst job ever), got a diagnosis (don't ask), entered the dating world—underwent a fatal attraction (sadly, not in a movie).

My faith had opened to bad reviews.

I misplaced my identity as I lost mask after mask—in the mirror nothing was left but eye-sockets and grin of a skull taunting— "who do you think you are?"—I searched—I tried a new thing or two—but most days just stood motionless as a picture of a guy waiting for Godard...and then CLUNK!

An anvil landed on my head!...and I knew at once—this fantastic shitshow was, in reality, the cartoon—between the double features of my life.

Oh, I heard a chorus of skeptics doubt:
"Just how Daffy Goofy Porky can one get?"
But, in the words of the master:
"The cinema is truth at twenty-four
frames per second,"

For I had passed on—between the worlds
I saw the light—I yielded,
turned towards it—entered it—squeezed
as it narrowed into a beam high
up a wall in the dark
I looked back and could see,
screened into Panavision:

COMING SOON

It was not my time.

So, I left the shreds of my past
on the cutting room floor, and
moved into a trailer on the lot.

FILM LOVERS ARE SICK PEOPLE

said Francois Truffaut, so
I wandered with him from wilderness
to the Valhalla of Cinema:
Facets Multimedia.
I entered to strains of Wagner.
I spent my last hundred bucks on a ticket package and
blissfully dissolved into my obsession-of-choice.
Under cover of a beret, I read *Cahiers du Cinema,*
cigarette dangling from unkissed lips.
And, oh, how I feasted those days!
French new wave for breakfast; Russian montage for lunch;
German expressionism, a heavy dinner...and, always,
the grainier the better.
I fattened up on jujubes, chuckles, m&ms.
And, at last, I had found God...he's

the concession guy who pours the butter on your popcorn.

I pack a viewfinder every day.

LIGHTS! ACTION!

You see, it's all just screenplay—and it's

COMING SOON!

THE RETURN OF THE PROJECTIONS

Starring Me, You, and
The Host of Heavenly Players—
(Any resemblance to real persons
is purely intentional)
directed by:
the MGM Lion
   (roars twice)

STUDY IN RED

Above us
El trains groan,
hauling the employed—
the old man caught me watching
him eating fries
from the wastebasket
one by one slowly
tasting each moment
purely as the broad
whiteness of beard
covering his chest
seeing me seeing him he
performs, mimes
the gentleman at buffet, picks
with delighted surprise
a cup half-full
of Hawaiian punch
meets my eyes with proud smile
of a knowing player
urging the moment
he lifts a toast
heaves it back
missing his mouth

splashing
red
all over white
in beads
drips and streaks
true as any thrown
stroke
of Franz Kline—
Art
forged by hunger—
untaught as thirst—

SUPPERS

Do this...

Da Vinci paints a moment
at the table
in the upper room

two men reach
for the same dish
the salt is spilt—
a betrayal divulged

the next day
they both die

the infant kingdom
impaled
its truth and its bearers
flung by the breach—
they land
in disjointed threes
with gestures wild,
the grasping
of refugees

yet their center,
Jesus, sits
a pyramid
a single eye
sees, upon
the table set,
a cup of wine...

in memory...

Warhol paints DaVinci.
Bold. Huge. Twice.
he joins these two
last suppers into one
vast canvas,
horizon-wide,
then conceals them
under a painted skrim
of army camouflage
of dark jungle green

facing this work—
one stands
small and misplaced
close to defeat—recruited
to scavenge its breadth and depth
for bits of the world's
new story—as much
as hunger and paltry insight
can digest—

invited,

yet we arrive
so hidden from the supper—
and suppers
hidden
from us

B-SIDE

a song is anything that can walk by itself/i am called a songwriter. a poem is a naked person...some people say that i am a poet
—Bob Dylan; (liner notes to *Bringing It All Back Home*)

At the coffeeshop, about to scrap my Bob Dylan poem,
I meet a guy who wrote three Dylan poems.

So, on cue, I recall
that sudden June—
the jukeboxes turned fierce—
and I, pink, mute, smart—
the only beginner in town;
ripe and alert for the word;
but after every captured answer
they changed the question.
In a dark living room
I got laid, all right
night after night
in front of speakers...
Bose, my sexy twins—
then the turntable spun me
back home—to Marshall Field's
8th floor, LPs—

in the glass listening booth
through made-to-wear earphones,
I was dealt
the Joker with electric hair,
cufflinks and cat—
a gotta-serve-somebody glare,
his all-nightlong-lyrics
lit fuses
in my brain—

how does the heat—
the <u>*real*</u> *heat—*
feel?—

and my whole terrain—
bombed away
leaving grey-matter craters
only the years would sow—
ever so slowly
yellow with
wildflowers.

CHAMBER MUSIC

Down on the stage
The Grateful Dead

survivors jammed
dancing below in clouds.

The 12-steppers,
circled on the hill

to summon sober stories...
hard to hear—

so our faces recall
the deaths: childhood,

Jerry
and the others

who passed
earlier by and left us

here
immersed in endless verses—

Ragtime—
wavelengths stretch

to the nearest dark star
and back again.

DAVID'S HOUSE

Zeus— afire inside Mnemosyne—Both:
I pray: bless this poem.
Sunrise to sunset my heavenly house
Rises brick by brick choirs of angels
Always providing sing each into being

Hear!—some are recalled:
your smile meets with mine...
last night and tonight an angel sleeps with me
Pizzas extra large! long-distance running
Forests, forest streams! and always, music!

Music: food of love! strings are tuning up
the lights are dimming baton lifted, waving—
take me out to the— fly-overs at games
cartoons at movies the virtues of dogs
making out with girls formed by Jesuits

travelling Europe windows of glass stained
fathering my sons memories of mom
psychotherapy— here's to the future
Welcome Rolling Stones! Dylan rolling on—
The Nibelung Ring—the cycles within:

the Jets and the Sharks
under the highway—sure I'll show up to
make it a fair fight—
and something's coming— so much shit resolves!
experience Now—

once more—an encore! cemented in place
nominate this poem best musical score
Master of nothing
led me through this house my name is David
I know I am loved

THE GHOST OF ELECTRICITY HOWLS

After Bob Dylan

After this poem
I will burn her pictures I will—
I swear on this unpublished manuscript.

—transient as—
wallpaper peeling in
this cheap room
these succeeding stanzas
visions of Jacqueline—

Once, in Florence, I penned
a life's devotion to Beatrice—
pilgrimaged and placed it by her tomb
in a basket there filled
with hundreds.

I wrote
in smoke—

Once, at the Green Mill,

I was heckled
for sounding like Alan Ginsberg
Howl! Howl! they howled

I edited
revelations—

Then in dream-time
she proved
unhinged—

movers hauled
furniture
and my drafts
out the door

I wonder when
Jacqueline and I
are but skulls
in our plots—
will we remain—
electric

LC

for *Leonard Cohen*

a hundred floors above me
and one above despair
I overheard

three minor chords
through pure
December air

there is no denouement
there is no finish line
there's only where the body is:

the dark at its shore
the radius of flame
the ground
under its knees

it endures
in four-four time
in what it reaps

jammin'

the way
down

Boogie Street

SATISFACTION AT SEVENTY

I know it's only rock n'roll

The climb up the ramps to the top
of Soldier Field
we touch the columns
massive as hubris—here
is the cusp:
dark and deep Michigan waves
greet the glorylit Chicago skyline
below a near-full moon just arrived
to join the few, the brightest stars

this June I'm seventy
the sky the stage my venue—
enter
the Rolling Sones
again, the dream
conjured

Mick the magic Jagger
our knighted
trickster-king
swagger-struts

lights the way
his lips love
the microphone
hips thrusting the same moves
that 54 years ago
just a mile down the lakefront
pre-schooled me in sex
then my dad drove us home
hey hey hey—
that's what I say
again the next year
I drove my car
my girl
my Marlboros:
I can't get no...

right now the hard rock
heart of stone drives
into the rage
behind the blues—
that's where
we painted it black
Brian the first martyr
as the muse of blues turned her smile
upon the glimmer twins—
Keith always-take-candy-from-strangers Richards
the lines in their faces—ravines
etched through death

tonight from a random spin of songs
Monkey Man—
I've been bitten I've been tossed around
By every she-rat in this town, so

Let's spend the night together

once chosen,
a conduit of beauty
of soul never dies
that flame it burns it dances along
this highwire act stretched
over decades
in the fringe between worlds
Mick and Keith
intone into one mike
You can't always get what you want
then sing the one word of Mr. Jimmy and that was
dead

GATES OF EDEN

(Dylan:Beleckis)

Needing my cowboy angel still I come
when I can—ear buds these days
where we shared poetry the first time:

upon the beach where hound dogs bay
at ships with tattooed sails

At fifteen I lay, in my living room,
in front of the speakers
Heading for the Gates of Eden

Mahogany console,
the arm had the shape and tongue of a cobra,
hypnotic the spin of the turntable
the carpet moving under me
lifted along bass runs
and volume and treble on high:

the B-side of Like a Rolling Stone:
The truth just twists its curfew gull it glides

Submerged in imageries—
as wicked birds of prey pick upon
my bread-crumb sins

There I meet
the motorcycle black Madonna two-wheeled gypsy queen
in the glow between
muse and word—
all in all can only fall
with a crashing but meaningless blow

To the chords of this hymn—
Aladdin and his lamp
granting wishes
my youth could not express—
with Utopian hermit monks,
sidesaddle on the Golden Calf

To awaken to the play of music
the first time
with a new love
and her troubled dreams—
a foreign sun that squints upon
a bed that is never mine

A poet alone in a baptistry
leans on the font of *no words*
but these to tell what's true—

and,

there are no truths outside the Gates of Eden

DEAD & COMPANY

I found the yellow balloons
between sets—our sober meeting:
deadheads in love
with two worlds

Around us—thousands—
under summer sun—
our small circle,
on the hill,
arms entwined
proclaim tearfully
true stories.

From a cup
ashes are poured out;
powder
on the grass—

Overdose—
Ethan used his ticket
after all

We sang "Brokedown Palace"

Ethan made it to the show
In time for the encore—

mama mama many worlds I've known
since I first left home

Writing

BUDDHA'S BUSINESS...

It is said:
at birth
he dropped
from the womb
walking—sprouting
at each footstep
a lotus

believing—
is what I must
be about—

so I beg—
a bowl
in each hand

I reap—
perhaps—
poetry's first line.

EMILY

Midwife to death
and immortality
connoisseur of zones—

We are called to travel on, I
in this pure land of white
all the paths of our lives—
further—until
an end in sight—

In homage,
as brief as truth,
clear as fate's next step
I glean
as you teach—bright
in sunlight
at noon—

THE HOLY GHOST

You've never seen the spirit-bird?
"Holy" bothers you?
relax...show me
your kind of love...

or "Ghost," is it?—
still watching
those movies?
Ah, a *poet*—
exacting with the word...
write it for me—
the word for you
exactly true.

Listen...
light is its sky
all light
imagine sleep

without dream-light—
in each
barren night
wings color

your myth
a match struck
in such dark
is seen across

midnight sky—
sunlight bakes earth
into life—
every photon
        chants
                enlightenment

IN THE ZONE

at the coffeeshop—
my writing buzz
gets highjacked
by one word
in red
on that guy's cap:

HIROSHIMA

I muse—
elect
not to ask,

get back to
journaling
this morning's dream—

the enemy,
gunshots
across the battlefield—
unarmed
exposed—

I decide
I stand
raise my hands—

slow walk

into the midst
of the fray

I look up,
watch
the play of sun
calm ten
trembling fingers—

up through

the vacuum

in blue

that blue—

the brink
of dream

I KNOW THE TRUTH

(after Marina Tsvetaeva)

An author sleeps with me every night—
sifts the falsehood of the day away
whispers in my ear:
I dare you to be happy

With intimate palette the dream
is colored, the players invited
to script the present act of life
every day, an epic of play

I trusted the poets, diffusers of the real,
more than Generals,
more than lovers, more than
books and buildings of revelation—

the adepts, purveyors
of the word who steer us
through starlit sleep christening
constellations on the way

I cannot be alone for I nightly hear
in lyrics or in din, precisely what
needs to be known,
escorted safely home

LITANY

"Pray tell me, what is your nectar?"
the poet asked

In the name of the One,
the flesh, the word—

Bees of the spirit let us gather
holy mothers rock me
muse from the agency sing
milk of paradise pour another
separated at birth find me
tower of ivory
Angels of Rilke shock me
Singular vessel of devotion
in seventeen syllables speak as One
mysteries of joy feed me
stone sinking down the Challenger Deep sound for me
House of gold
dreams from my hammock
stretched between stars light the way
undoer of knots free us
singular vessel of devotion
solstice of every winter

wonder of my sons pray pray
blue whale vomit us
on shores of sorrow
dharma bums dervishes ex-drunks storm on
we pray
cracked bells resound
washed-out trumpet blast this wall blast
all the walls
of all the diseased and the fallen
compasses all synchronize
point to exodus—
withdrawal unprayable
the poem unwritten
groaning
baptism of lesser gods
it's all
straw and pollen
oh virgin of virgins mother us
another son

NECTAR

What is your nectar?
a poet confronted me.
Name, my friend, the thirst that fires thirst.

the old answers flared:
—the foam the cold of Dortmund brews
—the hot-snake throat of hashish
—a spoonful of junk about to boil

then came a day
I tossed
a bottle from that shore—
LOST
I wrote—
nothing more...

                            * * *

today I know
it is a duo
the Beautiful—
the Word—

every moment
they mate—

they pollinate—

and, my friend,
this pen,
sweetly decrees:

DRINK! DRINK!

for all else
is straw.

SMITHY

This much I knew:
a horseshoe is like a poem—
you can't get far without one

So I built a shop of wood,
painted a sloppy sign:

    WORDSMITH:
    Horseshoes for the soul

Planted a tree—chestnut

One by one...they crawled in
climbed in, slid or tramped in
blindfolded
hungry as ghosts

Hard and fast all day long
the bellows roared
the forge flared
radiant orange

Poems cleaved poems fused
through times and time
the folks were fed
with rhymes and rhyme

Today, they walk upright
freed from their lack
clear-eyed and bright
they come once—they come back

Now I rest more than work—
the tree is tall, under its spread
I watch the busy squirrels
gather and bury, bury and gather

SUPERMAN—

the parallels are uncanny
like him, as my planet's about to explode
My loving mother and father
rocketed me towards earth
toward green and blue earth—

I landed on a farm
in Kansas
into the thankful arms
of childless Ma and Pa Kent—
(I can't help it if I'm lucky)

I grew up mild-mannered,
and very good
I like to: leap tall buildings
report things, spring into action
change my clothes in phone booths
yank off my glasses at critical moments,
and hold them pensively—

Look—up in the sky—
it *is* a bird—
but down here

I create metaphors
more powerful
than a psycho killer
faster than my red speedos
able to eat all the buffalo wings
and stick around—

my poems all —
super-profound.

TURNING SEVENTY

For the poets in my group, whom I love.
Whether I would love you if you did not
write poetry, is uncertain.

I tried and I tried to write a poem called "Turning Seventy,"
but stalled after:
"Birds are suddenly very interesting to me."
until seventy-two...
turning seventy takes a long time.

Some strange birds fly over me right now
a flock of insights:
some droppings...

I have transcended embarrassment.
Irascibility is fun.

I am a tree of life.
My deepest hair-thin roots
still drink through the humus
of first love lost.
An angel with a drawn sword guards me.

Seventy/scene four—take one:
On the way to Jupiter:
...the computer HAL singing
Daisy, Daisy, give me your answer true...
while being powered down by Dave.

Power naps have replaced dime bags.

There's more than one stain on my shirt.

The monsters of nightmares past have morphed
into disconcerting tribulations indecipherable as ever.

The peace beyond understanding remains beyond;
but my heart pumps blood and love.

I invite you all
to my one-billionth breath party.

The spooks, haunting this house—
lame as a William Castle movie;
mysterious sounds in the night—
now come from my body.

There's more than one stain on my pants.

I wonder what's in store for Dave beyond Jupiter?

Maybe I should join
a new souls' support group.

Beauty is Truth—Keats to the Kingdom—I
cherish you poets all.

I found the pearl beyond price, and buried it...
uh, somewhere around here...

Recalling in the midst of an animated description
that I've already told this person the same story with
the very same humorous emphasis.

My father at this age raised roses, his "babies."
Poems are offspring, counteracting
the beguiling temptation of inertia.

Fortinbras, awaiting his cue in the wings, nods off.

This far up the mountain,
the air is thin—
the vista is glory.

There's more than one stain on my shirt.

WARNING

You—
do not read this poem—
yes, you—
life doesn't hide
in your metaphors

every dream you slept away
last night
knows you
more than you think—
maybe more
than you'll ever know

why is your crawlspace
stuffed with sacks
of unopened letters?

and by the way—
existentialism
is a fire hazard

the world-dream
blazes on—

and here
you stand
lookin' down at
a smartphone

did Beauty
text you back?
Truth yawn
in your face?
hoping for
the right
hotline?

there's been a shift—
the wind is on to you

hurry—

pull pin
point at mirror
squeeze—

flames—

just singed
the edge of
the poem—

WRITERS' BLOCK

I sit unmoved with pen in hand;
When will my muse come around?
Like a bulimic about to hurl,
I've got to get this down.

Outdoors

ANOTHER MOVEMENT

I sit on a shoreline of boulders—
sweepings from some glacier—
as a sun climbs into an orange dawn
to play upon the waves.
Suddenly—a breach
of countless swifts—half fly low
and lower to skim to
a stop afloat.
Half fly on
upward—
arc slow miles
of loop—over again they glide
wings out
to rain
upon themselves
in one periphery—
except for four—
four beats of wings regain
the sky and arrow west,
diminish in distance,
leaving behind

the flock poised
on lifts and drops
bright
under
a higher sun.

BOUQUET

the bees and I reap
in the garden of delight—
find first a dahlia
of kelvin floodlight
a love in mist
for crown center then
encircle with seraphim of bounce
pink flame inpatiens
where dangles
the onyx red ornamental pepper—
Do Not Eat Thereof—
in brazen strides a Scarlet O'Hara morning glory
upstages the double hot cherry zinnia—
meanwhile beware
the blue false indigo creeps—its
pollen potent as the
the torch Mexican sunflower—
they stalk and grape
hyacinths scatter for cover

an electric pink cordyline breathes into
the lips of rocket red snapdragon—
the petunia sisters,

demure wave purple feigns nonchalance
but tidal wave silver flirts
heats it on high
for the eager Himalayan blue poppy—
then—in a splash the flamenco
orange coneflower succumbs
to bluecrown passionflower—
beauty and beauty
conmingle—come
in colors
everywhere
butterflies
and I cast
into abandon...

replete with zest
we all lie...ah,
melandpodium lemon delight!

TREE

The days will return
chlorophyll will again green forest-wide
the weathered trunk, another eon—
a new river etched in its map—

Traces of duration—cycled
times and time for
forestfuls of leaves
fallen and seasons of humus.

Roots coming, reaching, flushed by earthworms
across currents, sucking of rain-wet to the chant
the chant of the soil, quiet as, holy quiet as
a feather worn above.

Night keeps vigil, enduring as
the eroding coffin lid.
Above, the tree-leaves blend a canopy
upholding its charge

to accept nests, to shed seeds.

AUTUMN CREEK MEDITATION

An afternoon walk along my creek;
seeking repose until allured
by whisperings through a shoreline grove
to a sunlit clearing.
I take a seat on thick grasses sloping
into water's edge.
Here, the wide shallows rush
the flowing of the waters around a bend.
I breathe in lotus—the current
compels my gaze and I see
a streaming appear through groves
overhanging each bank, swerve around me,
and disappear into shade of canopy downstream.
The trees and sky project
themselves, spirited in seagreen,
upon the quivering watertop
greens rise into living blue
touching my feet—and in that blue,
clouds are centered by a rippling sunfire
scattering its flames.

Now and then cooling breezes stir
the trees—a disquiet, a trembling, then

a leaf in its time takes its leap—
wafted in spins and lifts then lights
upon the drift of that same seascape—
in surprise, finds itself—sailing—one in convoy—
a motley fleet!—leaves of sun-dazzled
yellow and gold and red and still-green—
born along a mazy route—
all one in seasonless current sailing down,
further down, to the river and on to the sea.

I see other leaves submerged,
and through the shallows
tumbled along, a procession
of baffled ghosts, unsoothed by
the one pace of the one watercourse...
yet drawn, further on,
downstream to the river.

Cragged bottom rocks,
rocks which pulse moss-green
trap these bright ones;
pinned in relentless current—
to be freed along, or at last
end in the slow dissolve—
but taken, always taken, down
to the river, to the sea.

MY CREEK

I breathe—the current
compels and I see
a streaming disappear down
into the shade of lush it engenders.
The trees and sky project themselves,
reflected greens rise into living blue.

And there, a fall of leaves—sun-dazzled
yellow and gold and red and still-green—
are born along a mazy route
a procession of baffled ghosts,
unsoothed by the one pace
of the one watercourse.

Cragged bottom rocks,
rocks to which long wavy mosses cling
and usher the drift of leaves towards
the slow dissolve—
taken, always taken
down, to the river,
down to the sea.

MY CREEK FROZE

My creek froze—
I knew it when
I walked on it and
heard the ice heave
like the belch of a whale
echo from the deep below
this sweeps me back—
or is it forward?—
to its summer world
the streambed...
in zazen
a bullfrog,
the color of muck, sits with me—
vigilant—
in the June breeze we see
with unmoving eyes
two dragonflies attach
in crazy dance
drop down
abed the surface tension they
mate and mate again—
skimmers swarm in zips and stops
thwart the current keeping

a playground
in place—
below them
the minnows
arrow all day
in and out of school—
a carp, fat and slow, comes
along, ignored,
with its big
mouth shoveling
on it goes...

here and now
over the bank
a bare willows hangs—
its lowest tips
suspended
inside that ice—
on it I stand—
rooted—
there's always a world
between the worlds.

NATURE POEM

The stream has crossed through my dream
the breath moves upon it, exhales
and its waters widen—a pond
a stillness that springs a world
I see from its shore as I sit
beneath one of the squat trees
lining the banks, under
branches bowing over the water
so low leaves here and there lightly kiss
their own very source

both eyes in zazen open to the sight
Of sunlit ripples reflected upward
from the black of earth through thickest foliage
root energy pulsing trunk and branch skyward
higher into the reach of green-
surging-to-blue horizon

in this silence I heard a drop—
a blackberry fell from its branch
perfectly caught on a lilypad—the strike
of a timepiece marking inscrutable flow

lilypads of this floating field
are so kindly placed they invited me
to cross in weightless step to another shore
skipping on the way over scattered crowns
of lily-white flames

and into this pool green as eden a mother swam
her seven goslings in easy
winding, a nibbling forage,
the slowest baby allowed
to dawdle far behind

through the thick stillness of surface mosses
a stirring from the algae-green below—
surfaces a mouth gaping yellow-pink
in sluggish close-and opening
a devouring carp swallows
in clumpfuls,
this lazy afternoon,
a bodyweight of foodstuffs

and then the silence erupts—
battling squawks—
angry birds, blackbirds, contest the space
around the berry tree—jumping flights
branch to branch the greenery thrashes
from fracas within—those
sweet greet-the-dawn calls now wicked
and high-pitched screeches
crossfiring threats to all invaders
including one awake—
seeing, hearing
under the tree.

SWARM

Sitting here for years
in the shade of this hawthorn
listening to endless arrival my creek
as it turns in lazy crescent;
timeless, the rushing song of its waters
timeless the churning, eroding of jutting rocks...

Wednesday last, floating just
above this streaming, I saw
a serpent—mystical, yes—
but potency in creation itself,
actual as eyesight

Gnats—of all things—but
in a swarm vast as millions
winding way back along the sweep
of the turn of the creek
the tiny wings of each
ignited by noonday sun
into a point of light bright
as any star of nightfall—
and not one insect ceased its flight
not one strayed beyond

the unison of compass
cued in concert by an unseen baton
to shape the life and pulse
of this creature of light
aglow from the teeming atomies within

as it slithered along its length
it puffed up wide then recoiled—
a body pulsing to prolong
this rapture of life

each insect ambled along back and forth,
up and down, while slowly progressing.
upstream—there each
turned around then
darted fast and straight
back through the meandering maze
downstream to the start—to turn again
to enter the lazy wayward forward flight—
over and over—
one in being—
borne all along the way
by the heart of summer wind

this carried on until my watch said go—
but since that day
I no longer walk away—
I just sit and look until I see
each one of the inhabitants
of this sagging skin
take flight.

TO THIS CREEK

Hike.
Alone...
to its secluded edge.
Sit...up close....
　　Wait.

The forest opposite—let it near
on ripples of seagreen through flashes of sunspots...
Hear the shallows rush around jagged rocks.
Soon, at your feet—minnows—
in schools of silver swimming upstream.
Skimmers defy the current—zipping back
to gather as one.
Motionless on a log
two—then three—turtles sunning;
meanwhile ants on task search the shore.
　　Wait.

The bullfrog's throaty appeal—
a cardinal trills his 4-notes—
Look—there—
A flair of red—

The hawk, on high,
circles and oversees.

You are an envoi
sent to caress
worlds—

Start here

Others

TITAN

                    UP
                  to the
                 warhead
                Flashpoint
               4,000 degrees
            for a hundredth of a
           second leaves charred
         flesh falling off in chunks
        (the first edge of the fireball;
         one of forty aimed at Moscow)
       Minutes before, 3 parachutes in quiet
       floatdown through clouds and miles
       blown westward by the willful winds
       towards 11 million breathing Muscovites.
       W-53 nuke, 9 megatons of genocide
       shot-putted from re-entry vehicle
       in upper atmosphere, which gunned
       off from stage two in late downward
       arc guided through Russian airspace;
       from its north pole apogee adrift between
       starry black above and white of polar ice
       in stillness over the turning world
       the quiet of balance riding the Tao
       latent like lightning…floating further
       in mach 3 silence after a hundred thousand
       pounds of thrust up, boosted over Yukon
       so high the horizon bends into earth's round
       swell heaved up to this threshold by
       LR 87 engine: half a million thrust-pounds
punches up a mile then another mile through clouds then
more miles—most of its heft burnt in first heave of launch
off thick steel. Titan throned in silo: god of war reigning
with leashed death high as a ten-story building packed with
twenty tons of fuel and savage machinery; its twin incurved
engines downward waiting caves, two bulging eyes of darkness
dotted with hundreds of tubes—and then—2 keys are turned—
Ignition: 2 tanks shoot gasses through into chamber igniting
Melee of jumping electrons—zillions of tiny explosions propel
in unified eruption the downburst fire-slam of thunder
against launch pad steel—and the god stirs, intent on death:

Aerozine 50	and	N204
exploding down	- and we have	lift
blast		off

APOGEE

Stage one shell, prostrate in Arizona desert;
stage two cast adrift in orbit over Siberia;
Re-entry Vehicle with payload,
a W-53 9-megaton bomb,
sits in still point of its apogee—
over a dangling earth—
neither ascent nor descent
but emptiness of the tomb
in sleep of that space, delta sleep—
below, a daughter of Moscow
lying blanketed—
her eyes twitch, and then again
with emerging dream, like
first words of a poem.

CEASEFIRE

Ceasefire—didn't you hear—
all warfare is accomplished

ceasefire—the last burning coal
of your leaving still glows

ceasefire—pry the heart open
then wave all thoughts white

cease that worn trajectory
fire the captor who keeps you hidden

quench the fire
behind desire

from water and earth and air
let your life transpire

DEEP CALLS TO DEEP

(Psalm 42:7)
You need to listen. Listen.
Hear the many calls of the one word.

Can't say "no" one more time—
you're done, done with saying no.

And you turned to your ghosts only to find
a ghost too is more than one person.

Glimpsed in a sudden poem,
you wrote:

The eye that seeks and the eye
That finds is the same eye.

Yes—now fly under mothlike stars
through leaves and fields,

listen to pheromones of sound, strains
plucked by ancestors and saints.

This is right hearing: open mind to mind.

FIRST LOVE

Jacqui
starred
from the footlights

by closing night we wore
each other's rings

three years later I gave
her a diamond—

flawless—but
she started seeing me

I was abruptly dumped—

one phone call
from forever to never

my dreamlife
she could not sever

in dream after dream
I walked her street

until
the day I heard
she dispatched
her spouse with
the same bite
that same
venom
swift like
a widow.

FLIGHT PATH

Sitting, meditating
from my balcony
I watch
the ascent of moon
through the summer night
huge, blood-orange
and fevered she swells
seizing the sky and holding
the city helpless under
a cast-down haze
thick like lava.
Chicago is choking
in orange smoke,
and the moon's gone mad—
the queen of night

I watched safely from my cushion
when—from the airport miles behind
a plane in takeoff
appears to rise—

straight up, like a rocket,
with flashing red and white wingtips

launched at that moon
a dreadful machine
in lethal stealth
on target
lunges up pierces
the moon's exact center
leaving a black, stark contrail
fierce it sliced
that moon in two.
Then flew on.

The trail it left moves
to the north, drawn
by an intake of breeze,
slowly over craters
and lunar seas, when,
another flight flashing
the same point
with course precise
as the blade of a compass
leaves her slashed—

and then, by the same breath,
follows the first
minutes and then
a third,
yes, again...

I bowed my head—

prayed for those
in three planes bound
for three cities—

a thousand sojourners soon
to lay in a thousand beds to dream
ten thousand dreams

but one or two or three
will dream
they are healed—
see in their sleep
that they have pierced the moon,
blinded the eye of a queen.

GREEN INTO BLUE

Green spools into blue,
always and alltimes. The ensouled—free

to seek its true cast. Upheld by
every breath, in the point, white and empty,

between exhale and inhale—just there—where color pours
and plays into portrait: a vagrant, in faded fatigues,

picks, with his good hand, french fries
from the trash on Wabash street;

as tossed scraps sustain enduringly,
like happenstance, like loaves.

The El, shouldered by girders of rust and green,
loops and rumbles by above...

"For madmen only" is etched
on the archway to middle-age—

and days, years, yes, decades, turn and turn,
spiraling to all topmost leaves.

SHOPPING

They were struggling
thrashing to get the
collapsible walker
tucked onto the store's cart
It kept slipping off
blocking the sliding door.
Grey-haired, feeble, he shakes,
drops his white and red cane
pushing from one side
as she, younger, tough,
yanking from the other—
they wrestle with
much tinny clanging—
and shoppers waiting
behind their carts
watch.

Just then
it falls back out—
blocking the door again...
amped up and frantic
over the rattle
of clashing effort she scolds:

uhhh—UHHHH—UHHHH!!
the stifled fuming
of a mute;
and a longer line
of eyes averting
piteous sight.

I wish I could load them up
and buy them a feast—
alms for pettiness
of my grievances;
from silence a prayer
for us all—
up the aisle
with efficient roll:
oatmeal, a jar of olives...
I look back—
their empty cart still
at the start—
as she calmly raises choices one
by one up
to his eyes.

MAXIMUM SECURITY ZAZEN

Eyes open
the circle sees itself
twenty men in beige get-ups
D-O-C across their backs
shoes black, or white, bright as new—
no dirt, no strings, no distance.

We sit   breathe,
reach—a tide
upon a shore—
what is owed
settles.

Palms surrender
on thighs; feet
plant on concrete.

This space, the "Chapel"
a rounded gym ascends
through tiers.
Those cells,
concrete-thick

time
harder
than the fall;
no clocks
in this tower of white.

Three south-siders
sit together;
three times twenty years
ago-three teenagers, three
sentenced
to life.

    Antoine
embittered—
twelve hours a day,
caged with
a cellmate's
foaming mouth
and reeking shits.

    Mick
polite, eager
with questions
about kundalini
and altered states.

    Johnnie
can't sit still—
says he's hopeful
about parole—
ten years from now

This morning, the hour
has passed
the guards are late—
we sit.

SIGNAL

I seized a cure I gulped
distance and speed—

got hooked on both—

waiting for the moment
my '64 Impala—

four on the floor—

chrome and leather
burned west across
the plains then
south into
foothills twisted
as lifeblood when

my Chevy
threw a rod
spat its oil
over Interstate Ten

so I hitched I hiked

I followed crows
and my thumb—right
through the real heat—

at the desert's edge
found myself
face-to-face
with a signpost

Welcome to Signal:

a brown street
between heaps
of collapsing wood

a store, a brewery,
thirteen saloons—

Signal, Arizona

SNOW IS FALLING OVER CHICAGO

And it is falling upon the landscape of time itself
through dark clouds blown down
athwart arctic winds of Canada.
It covers all green—the grass of lawns and parks—
the outfields and basepaths of northside
and southside; blankets beach after beach
of the people's lakefront to
sweep over the January ice of Lake Michigan

Upon the barn of Mrs. O'Leary—the burning—
and the next day—
the architects arrive—fire of beauty in their eyes
and plans to scrape the sky forever

Covers the grave of Mayor Cermak who took
a bullet for FDR
Joe E Lewis, who sang one night at the wrong club—
Capone, offended at the Green Mill, sliced his throat

Upon world war pilots training at Navy pier

Upon the stations hoisted

by girders—the El tracks of the Loop—
the circle, in fact, squared.
It is snowing in back-of-the-yards
Lincoln Meats, the last slaughterhouse

It snows upon the gangs of the ghettos
covers the guns and dealing
from the riotous beer and booze speakeasy
to drive-up bags of fentanyl delirium.
always sellin'—always buyin' what the folks are cravin'
while cops twirl batons

And gentrifiers bulldoze forever
their channel to downtown gold

The visionary gleam—the Machine
of democrats who run
the city that works—just slip the cash and
another win-win
covered up

Oh, fall and bless
every hood for every immigrant
speaking every language, longing for home—
rows of bungalos of tiny rooms—
but space profuse for a family
to learn not English, but American—
to live to die
to break bread to give thanks—
a short walk to church...or the corner bar.

And work—factories that turn out
anything you want

work and its yours
in this three-shift town

And the one blanket of white
in the outskirts shrouds the cemeteries
whose generations long dispersed—
in forgotten graves crammed
within falling fences
rest the builders of this city

The snow so deep
this year every year from the silent skies—
and more is coming—
so curse and shovel
the sidewalks and push stuck cars—
it's cold and good.

Fall, snow, fall—you can't stop
this city of beer-belly laughs
and sledge-hammer business
muscle and boots and
the big shoulders of character—
I will sing this song—
It's my kind of town

SOLSTICE

Winter is coming
breath steams through my scarf
slap my gloves, jog in place
a long night run
led to crossing the bridge
over this river—the jagged border
between two states

halfway across the walkway
of towering span of steel-and-cable hubris
I am drawn close to the edge

so high the vertigo
I grip the rail
I peer down—
vision deepens with plummet
into a canyon black
as creation's first day

headlights appear—I hear
the racing-drone of ten tons of truck
driven at speed man was never meant to go—
loud and louder— peaks

to assaulting roar
then quiet as taillights shrink away
into the howl of gusts of wind

I become still as next breath—hear
the faint rush of waves
icing slowly into silence;
and from that gorge—unbidden—
an impulse—as if spoken—
rises to my heeding:

go over
you can go over—

and I know three seconds
of freefall—three seconds to—
the end of time—the time of travail—
at impact—
upon those waves
spirit is yielded—seared
and shredded
and swept into its own
unending undercurrents—
consciousness of river becomes river—
the way to the sea
is the other side of sorrow

I step away...
I leave the night to its wiles—

pulled back
as I tried to pray
to this god of darkness—

but I can only hear
my own entreaty—
to the drawing near
of solstice

UP

the highest peak
in the range, two of us
rest for water, raise a toast
to the valley below
our wings
wrested away as we eye
the precipice above—
a throne of rock
eagle—worthy
awaiting

with a nod—
we're back to it—
the only course—
up

through the treeline
where roots mad with thirst
nurse the gaunt refugees
for up here
rock triumphed
and the king
sorely rations green

up
over boulders
we strain
each muscle each pain
a stretch a grasp a thrust
harder higher
until we perch
just under the summit
we face
one more test-
a span of granite
broad and worn slick
steeply sloped
its edge—a plunge
onto spine-cracking
crags

at its top
in a rush of zeal
I missed the rope
to short-cut across—
inching on my back
then— on a film of shale
I slipped then
I slid—

down—

within a foot
of the fall
bare rock
grabbed me
to a stop

I looked at Doug
our wild-eyed
terror shot down

through granite
all the way
and
the mountain

erupted

with
laughter

VOID PHOBIC

—or not
to be—

crossing the night
on a wave
from the sea
where myths go
to drown—

dying
can be done
but this flame—
blown out

annuls
analogy

THIS JUST IN

Latest muse from temp agency fired for engendering twaddle.

Defective Louisville slugger acting slug-like

Church-mouse suddenly and inexplicably loud-mouthed and skeptical

Universal query "How could they do that to me?" definitively answered.

Getting lost determined to be most effective means of finding oneself

TRUTH OUTS after centuries of deceit, sham, mal-intentioned guile, pretense, stupidity, and general inanity, Wisdom has triumphed and we now inhabit the world of Truth

ANTIMUSE ON DEVOURING RAMPAGE over half the poets in Southern hemisphere reported missing or dead

GOLDEN CALF FOUND Thursday, as road-kill on highway 47 in rural Minnesota

HE NOT BUSY BEING BORN IS BUSY DYING

REINCARNATION PROVEN Resemblance of salamander to Grandma Aikens too uncanny to be chance

CHARACTER IS DESTINY death-row oddballs and cut-ups unanimous in assessment

Chinese leadership warns that further U.S. sanctions against North Korea will result in shipments of less auspicious fortune cookies

ARK LANDS SAFELY ON MOUNT ARARAT. Noah, wife, two of every animal on earth reported in good health. Rainbow seals eternal covenant with deity.

DAVE BELECKIS, HUMMINGBIRD

You might say I was born obsessed.
Yes, a hummingbird...a cross between Antman
and Batman—the superhero of the avian world.

Today, through the miracle of genetic engineering,
speeded up to a thousand beats per minute
I have placed an order to be transformed...
I'm waiting to hear back.

Our little bird weighs the same as a nickel...
re-proportioned to my six-foot frame
I am now a svelte two-and a-half pounds.

I can fly—don't need a cape, my wings flap
fifty times per second...
tiny copter I whir
hover above in tiny sky
backwards fly—
very handy when you're me...

I'm attracted to bright colors, especially red...
you should see my living room...

I know your face, and
I'm smarter than you—I can recall
every flower I've ever sipped...
and where I found it.

Each year, I migrate
to the moon
without refueling.

If I catch you
where I eat—
beware—
this beak.

So—here I am—
Ta-Ta!—
here I'm not

in a flash
you can't see—that's me
in my tree.

AT THE OL' BALLGAME

the June sky darkens
but I got tickets to illumination
transported to a needed
change of view
a city within a city
this magic-valley below
infield mystical green outfield
perfect flat and glowing—
hundreds of floodlights—not
one burned out
two of us share this upper-deck magic it's
three outs in the seventh
so, with the carefree crowd
we heartily sing

I don't care if I ever get back

Really—
for nine innings I got it all
in my White Sox T:
fans who are happy
my wife cheering too
sauerkraut on my brat—

and umpires to boo—

Let the sublime and ironic
dour tomorrow—did
you know...

The ball takes
half a second to go 60 feet 6 inches
a 34-inch bat gripped by hands
with .75 second reaction-time
up down in away or fast—
a swing a crack—a launch into the matrix
space-time-ball
limitless the outcomes
from low and away
to home-run fireworks
to evenings like this
all over- October.

JELLOMAN

Exploding- EXPLODING
around me—constant—
close—closer
every time—
dirt flying—
meteors zero in—
finding me—
before I crack—I
floodlight night clouds
with the alarm:
J-E-L-L-O
And, quick as a shudder
a super-shape
congeals
before me,
lime-green J on his chest
a cherry-red cape
muscled as a jellyfish
it's JELLOMAN!
Before my eyes
he molds into
a star of orange—
he cools,

my panic cools—
"I want to die"
now just a thought—
a jiggle in time
as the memory
of table at holiday.
In the center
he lazed
seen inside his
limpid form:
cherries, pineapple and nuts
the family, my cradle
of neurosis,
eyes
our dessert
in the room
we always have
for jello.

ME AND MY SHADOW

The sun before its nightly set
poured its orange
over the dried
browns of November prairie, as well
as my dark thoughts.

Startled then—out of myself—
to my left—another runner on
my long loop through the meadow—
caught up with swift stride
and near-perfect form—a lusty svelte—so
transparently flaunting his absence
of body fat, and, by the way, he
ran perpendicular and was a good
twenty-five feet long as he
breezed right through and over tall
and dead grasses and plants.

He swung ahead of me and kept the pace along
as I stabbed his backside with deadly glares.
The uphill slope shrunk him to more my size and
I was stuck with him and his head
way too close to mine—

Hey what's your problem?
I shouted but
he answered with silent contempt
and haughty refusal to put
distance between us. He swung
to my right in obstinate orbit.
I ignored my wrath and groaning bones
and pounding heart when I spied
his anorexic torso glide
with grace through marsh reeds
and cattails and his head float along
on a pond's still waters...
Why oh why can't I do that?
Downhill sloped faster, so
Unable, desperate to gain
even one step on this foe
in panic I tried to pray this rival away—
oh please get behind me—
—and then he did—
lagging, then trailing thirty feet and
farther, forty fading to fifty
forsaking the visible
as the final sliver of sun succumbed,
he, then the meadow
slipped away from the day—
leaving me now alone
to walk my path
through a darkness
all my own.

OZ

With a HA-HA-HA

I had dribbled away my teens; too short
and stuck out of bounds in converse all-stars
a wind found me and spun me fast, then faster
into a cranial hurricane that blew
me out west to the mountain to the desert
and into daylong night where the ghosts of saguaros
roamed—drugs spun my faith into straw—
a road appeared as
emboldened crows picked away
every brick glowed acid-yellow—
compulsed I was
to follow follow follow follow—

and a HO-HO-HO

flying monkeys cackled away my sleep—
nowhere between night and day could I hide
I drank for courage and drank my courage away
I groped with little people in their cheap hotel—
Grafitti sprayed over the entrance:
SURRENDER YOU PRETENDER

Nothing more green to be seen and
all this time the wizard watching, bemused

and a couple of TRA-LA-LA'S

after nine months I despaired...I decided to die
then before my eyes, all wickedness melted
into a puddle—I stepped over—swooned at a doorway
saw the wizard face-to-face
the game itself revealed—

I awoke in a stream wading eastward
just one of many dreamers of light—they
shoved me rudely, because I had dared too much,
up to the front of our march
and we all resumed.

that's how we laugh the day away
in the merry old land of Oz!

Fifteen Little Poems

Quotable

"I Die Daily."
 —*Paul of Tarsus*

"Me Too,"
 —*Dave*

Solution to Yesterday's Crossword from the Hades' Daily Herald

D

IT

D

HAPPEN

T

Since his Annie—passed on—as a wind

from a doorway to the darkness blows hard in

Cut your ties
while still alive—
no ghost can raise
your axe

In the poetry casino,
high-stakes dice—
one throw—
lose it all
—or—
write it now

In the mail

I travelled to where
the poets go—

it's nowhere in space
yet always so near

thus, to the visible, we post
these cards, which say

wish you were here.

Of what I seek
deep in—
my cracked
bathroom mirror:

my creek with
  loveflows—
    neverslows—even
      for a kiss

I know of something that every time
will make you smile—
so certain that I dare to wager—
so please, lay down a bundle—
and activate my
zygomaticus major

The worthy sisters taught us well;
I'm on my way to heaven—
for they made sure
I did my time—in hell

After heavy rain,
I toss earthworms
from the sidewalk—
back home

So vexed,
to see
my faults in others—
but will I ever
learn to leave
a crime-scene—
untorched?

Returning
to these timeless woods—
I find
my small
waterfall—
falling
still

The octopus
slithers back
into the coral
guards
the pulse of the poem.

"I am who I am"
Proclaimed
the burning bush—
Well,
So am I, big guy

Entry:

my mother's journal
1937

Boat ride with Bruno—

Scrumptious!

ACKNOWLEDGMENTS

My heartfelt thanks to my family and to the many sober friends, poets, artists, writers and teachers who have inspired, supported, and guided me. I am deeply grateful to my wife, Joan, for her wise and caring listening.

ABOUT THE AUTHOR

David Beleckis grew up in Marquette Park, Chicago. He attended Loyola University and the University of Arizona. He has worked as a hospital and hospice chaplain, an addiction counselor, baker, photographer, and, most formatively cabdriver. His work—across streets, clinics, and hospital rooms—reflects a calling and the belief that every life holds a sacred story worth hearing. Dave is retired and lives in River Forest, Illinois with his wife Joan.

www.ingramcontent.com/pod-product-compliance
Lightning Source LLC
Chambersburg PA
CBHW071721120626
46550CB00001B/323